SPACE MYSTERIES

MIKE GOLDSMITH

 RAINTREE
STECK-VAUGHN
PUBLISHERS

A Harcourt Company

Austin   New York
www.steck-vaughn.com

spinning through space

SPACE
MYSTERIES

Other titles in the series: • Comets and Asteroids • Constellations • The Earth • The Moon • The Solar System • Space Travel • The Sun

Published by Raintree Steck-Vaughn Publishers, an imprint of Steck-Vaughn Company

Library of Congress Cataloging-in-Publication Data
Goldsmith, Mike.
Space Mysteries / Mike Goldsmith.
    p.   cm.—(Spinning through space)
    Includes bibliographical references and index.
    ISBN 0-7398-2745-6
    1. Outer space—Juvenile literature.
    [1. Outer space.]
    I. Title. II. Series.

Printed in Italy. Bound in the United States.
1 2 3 4 5 6 7 8 9 0 05 04 03 02 01

CONTENTS

THE UNKNOWN UNIVERSE

The Big Bang

The universe is full of mysteries, and the biggest of all is—where did it come from? Scientists don't yet know just how the universe began, but they do know roughly *when* it happened: between 12 and 15 billion years ago in a gigantic burst of energy called the "Big Bang."

There are more stars in the sky than all the grains of sand on all the beaches in the world. Most of these stars are too far away to be seen from Earth.

Gradually, the universe expanded and cooled, and matter started to form into huge clumps. This happened through the force of gravity. (Gravity is the pull that everything in the universe makes on everything else; it keeps the planets going around the sun and holds us to the Earth.)

▼ Millions of years after the Big Bang, thickening clouds of matter became the birthplaces of the first stars.

Slowly the clumps became thicker and hotter, until, in places where there was enough hot material crushed together, stars formed.

▲ A distant part of the universe, in which many galaxies can be seen. Some of them are so far away that their light takes 10 billion years to reach the Earth.

Galaxies

Stars are grouped together in huge collections, called galaxies, which contain between a million and a trillion stars. Galaxies are grouped into clusters and clusters into superclusters. Astronomers can see galaxies billions of light-years away.

On a very clear night, you can see up to 2,500 stars.

There are mysteries about all sorts of things in space, from the moon to the far reaches of the universe.

Near Mysteries

The moon is the nearest natural object to Earth. No one is sure where it came from, though scientists know it is similar in age to the Earth. One theory is that a planet-sized object crashed into the Earth more than four billion years ago. A chunk of debris was torn away from Earth and formed the moon.

The closest star to the Earth is the sun. From the Earth, it looks much brighter than anything else in the sky. Yet the source of its light was only discovered in the 1930s. The sun is made mostly of a gas called hydrogen, which is so hot and squashed at the sun's center that it is transformed into another gas, helium. This process releases enormous amounts of heat and makes the sun shine.

◄ The surface of the moon. The craters were made by the impact of enormous chunks of rock billions of years ago.

▲ A spiral galaxy
1.4 billion light-years from
Earth, with a quasar at the
center.

Far Mysteries

Some of the farthest objects known are quasars (short for quasi stellar objects). Quasars are incredibly bright objects—millions of times brighter than the sun—that give out intense radiation. They are found in the centers of distant galaxies, more than 3 billion light-years away. Scientists are not sure where quasars get all their power.

The expansion of the universe means that all distant objects are moving away from us. The most distant quasars are moving away at more than 174,000 mi (20,000 km) every second!

MYSTERIOUS NEIGHBORS

Venus

Venus, the nearest planet to the Earth, is easy to see in the night sky—yet it was a mystery until very recently. This is because it is covered with thick clouds that hide the surface from us.

The temperature on the surface of Venus is about 896°F (480°C). The intense heat and the dense, destructive atmosphere of Venus make it an inhospitable planet.

It used to be thought that Venus might be covered with water, overrun by dinosaurs, or inhabited by an advanced civilization. In fact, the surface of Venus is much hotter than an oven, and no life—or water—can exist there. The high temperature is caused by a gas in the Venusian atmosphere called carbon dioxide that traps the sun's heat.

◄ A radar map of the surface of Venus. It has been colored to show how the planet might look if we could see through the clouds.

On Venus, the sky is orange, and it rains sulfuric acid—which boils away before it reaches the ground.

In the 1970s, probes from Earth landed on Venus, and, in the 1980s and 1990s, further probes made detailed observations of the planet. They discovered that Venus has more than 50,000 volcanoes and a very strange surface. Scientists are still trying to understand it. It may be that sometimes there are volcanic eruptions on Venus so huge that the whole planet is covered with lava.

Another of the mysteries of Venus is the incredibly strong wind encountered by space probes in the upper atmosphere of the planet.

▼ Maat Mons, a 5-mi (8-km) high volcano on Venus, mapped by radar from an unmanned spacecraft

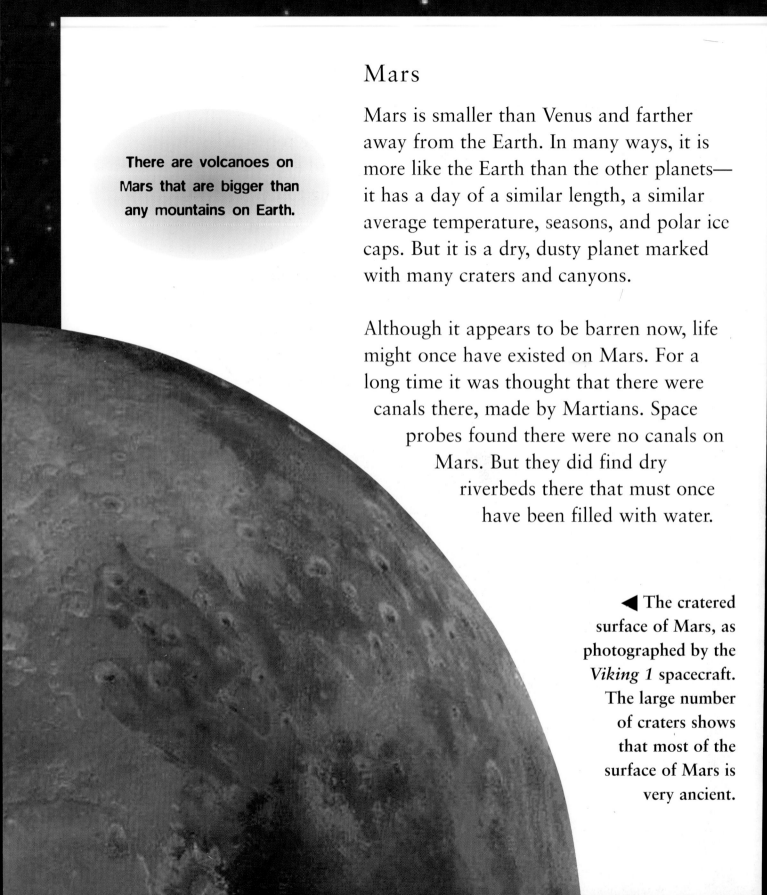

There are volcanoes on Mars that are bigger than any mountains on Earth.

Mars

Mars is smaller than Venus and farther away from the Earth. In many ways, it is more like the Earth than the other planets—it has a day of a similar length, a similar average temperature, seasons, and polar ice caps. But it is a dry, dusty planet marked with many craters and canyons.

Although it appears to be barren now, life might once have existed on Mars. For a long time it was thought that there were canals there, made by Martians. Space probes found there were no canals on Mars. But they did find dry riverbeds there that must once have been filled with water.

◀ The cratered surface of Mars, as photographed by the *Viking 1* spacecraft. The large number of craters shows that most of the surface of Mars is very ancient.

Vikings Invade Mars

Even to the naked eye, Mars looks red: why? Because it is rusty! There is a lot of iron in the Martian soil, and the atmosphere of Mars turns it into rust.

In the 1970s, it became clear from the *Viking* robot probes that, if there had ever been life on Mars, it was going to be difficult to find. One of the *Viking* probes carried out experiments to look for signs of living creatures in the Martian soil. One of the experiments gave a positive result—but most scientists think it detected strange chemical reactions rather than life. Some scientists think there is a chance that life-forms exist deep underground.

▼ The Martian landscape. On a winter day, the rocks are covered with frost that melts away when the temperature rises.

RIDDLES OF THE GIANT PLANETS

Our solar system contains four giant planets: Jupiter, Saturn, Uranus, and Neptune. There is something mysterious about each of them, which scientists have found difficult to explain.

Jupiter

Jupiter has what looks like an enormous red eye, called the Great Red Spot. The spot is more than twice as big as the Earth. Some people used to think it might be a gigantic red mountain. In the 1970s, space probes proved that it is really a hurricane that has been raging for centuries. Scientists don't know how much longer it will last.

Saturn

Astronomers have known for a long time that Saturn has rings around it, but recently they have found that all the other giant planets have them, too. They know the rings are made of dust and rocks, but they have so far found it impossible to explain the shapes and sizes of some of them.

Uranus

The odd thing about Uranus is that it rolls along on its side. It is tilted more than 90 degrees to its orbit around the sun. This means that on parts of the planet that face away from the sun, nights can last for nearly forty years.

▲ The Great Red Spot on Jupiter is a storm that has been going on for over 300 years.

Jupiter is so big that 1,300 Earths could fit inside it.

▲ The solar system with the sun at the center (not to scale)

Uranus may have been "knocked over" by a collision with an unknown object as big as a planet.

Neptune

The farthest giant planet, Neptune, has incredibly windy weather, like an everlasting hurricane. The *Voyager* probes found that all the giant planets are surprisingly stormy, but the weather on Neptune is the windiest of all. Neptune has a flow of heat from its core that warms the atmosphere from below and causes the strong winds. A storm system called the Great Dark Spot was discovered in Neptune's Southern Hemisphere in 1989, but it had vanished five years later.

Neptune is so far away from the sun that it takes 165 years to make one orbit.

Jupiter

Io

Ganymede

Callisto

Europa

▲ The planet Jupiter and its four largest moons. The images of the moons have been enlarged in comparison with Jupiter.

Some of the rings of the giant planets are kept in place by the gravity of tiny moons called Shepherds.

The giant planets have lots of moons, and some of them are very strange indeed.

Io and Europa

Jupiter has a moon called Io, on which a gigantic volcanic eruption has been seen. The whole surface of Io is often flooded with molten lava that hardly has time to set before more lava covers it again. Europa, another moon of Jupiter, is covered with ice. Under the ice, scientists think that there might be a huge sea stretching over the whole moon.

Titan and Iapetus

Saturn has a mysterious moon called Titan that is as big as a small planet. The atmosphere contains chemicals similar to those from which life was formed on Earth. It is so cloudy that only vague shapes can be seen on the surface. Another of Saturn's moons, Iapetus, is black on one side while the other side is as bright as snow. No one knows why.

Triton, one of Neptune's moons, has geysers that spout nitrogen gas.

Miranda

Uranus has a moon called Miranda that has a strange, jumbled surface. Astronomers think this moon may have moved too close to Uranus and been torn apart by the strong gravity of the planet. Afterward, the fragments gradually drifted together again.

▶ The surface of Titan, Saturn's largest moon, may look like this. Titan is the only other place in the solar system that might have oceans on its surface. But they would contain liquid methane rather than water.

SPACE RUBBLE

In addition to big things like planets, our part of the universe contains all sorts of smaller objects. Comets are a bit like giant dirty snowballs that make long journeys through the solar system. When they approach the sun, they grow tails of dust and gas. Occasionally they can be seen from Earth with the naked eye, looking like smudges of light in the sky.

Meteoroids are pieces of rock or grains of dust that travel through space, often in large groups. Once meteoroids enter the Earth's atmosphere, they burn up and are called meteors, or shooting stars. This is normally the end of them, but a few survive their fall through the atmosphere to land on the Earth. The lumps of rock that remain are called meteorites.

▲ Comets are made of dirty ice, mixed with dust and grit. They can be seen from Earth, but only when they have moved fairly close to the sun.

In 2000, it was discovered that Comet Hyakutake has a tail 340 million mi (550 million km) long—nearly four times longer than the distance from the Earth to the sun.

Danger from Space

Asteroids are like tiny planets, mostly found between Mars and Jupiter in a region called the Asteroid Belt.

The fall of an asteroid may have caused the mysterious death of the dinosaurs more than 60 million years ago. The crash may have thrown up so much dust that the sun's heat was blocked out. Then it became too cold for the dinosaurs to survive. An asteroid big enough to threaten the whole of civilization will probably fall on the Earth within the next few hundred thousand years. Astronomers are monitoring space for the approach of such objects.

▼ Most asteroids are found in a belt between the orbits of Mars and Jupiter. The largest is nearly 620 miles (1,000 km) across.

STRANGE STARS

The twinkling of the stars is caused by movements of the Earth's atmosphere—they don't twinkle when seen from space. But the light of some stars really does change.

One of the first of these "variable" stars to be discovered was Algol, the "Demon Star." This star takes a few hours to fade and brighten again. The cause of the changing light was a mystery for many years. But an astronomer discovered the reason in 1782—there are two stars orbiting one another and blocking each other's light.

Some stars, called RCB stars, almost vanish from time to time. Their light is blotted out by huge clouds of soot, formed by the stars themselves. RCB is short for R Coronæ Borealis, the name of the first star of this type to be identified.

▶ There are many pairs of stars that regularly block each other's light. They often appear very different in size, brightness, and color.

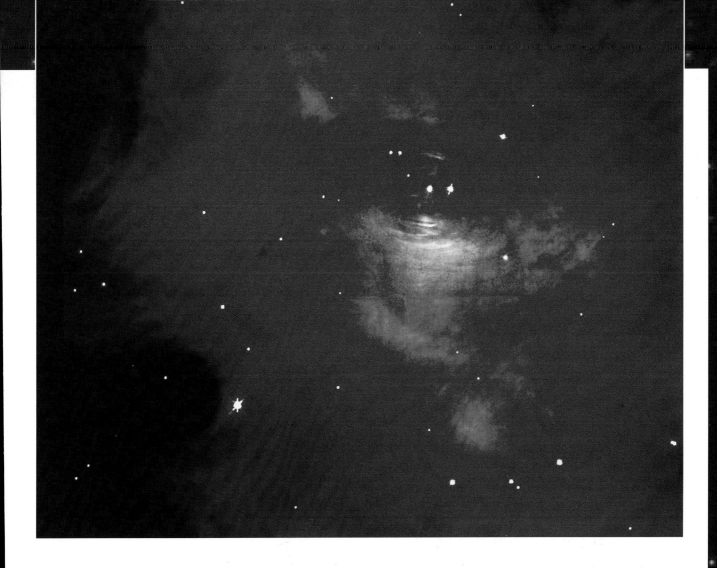

Exploding Stars

Sometimes stars explode. These stars, called supernovas, can be so bright that they outshine whole galaxies. These huge explosions can happen when massive stars run out of fuel and collapse. One supernova was seen by Chinese and Japanese astronomers in 1054 in the constellation of Taurus. Today, it is called the Crab Nebula, a bright, expanding shell of dust and debris with a pulsar at its center.

▲ The center of the Crab Nebula, the debris of a supernova explosion that was recorded nearly a thousand years ago

Lots of the atoms in your body were made in a supernova. The atoms were part of the gas cloud that formed the sun and the Earth.

Dead Stars

Only big stars explode when they run out of fuel. But when any star dies, some of the leftovers will remain as a lump of cooling matter: a dead star.

When a star dies it shrinks, because the material it is made of is crunched up very tightly. The more material a star contains, the more squashed together it becomes. In many billions of years, all that will be left of the sun will be a white dwarf. It will be so tightly packed that a teaspoonful will weigh more than an elephant!

A dead star can make a black hole. For this to happen, a quantity of matter at least three times the mass of the sun has to be squeezed into a space of only a few miles.

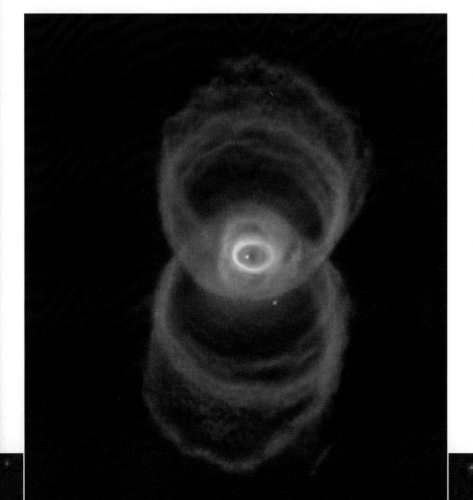

◀ The Hourglass Nebula, the remains of a red giant star. The bright spot near the center is a white dwarf.

▲ A spiral galaxy with a black hole at its core might look like this.

Black Holes

Some stars collapse when they run out of fuel and leave behind very strange objects. These objects have such an incredibly strong gravitational pull that not even light can escape from them. Because of this, they look black and are called black holes. Black holes are very strange, because no one really knows what happens when the pull of gravity becomes so strong. Although we cannot see black holes directly, we know they are there because material falling into them emits X rays that scientists can study.

If you fell into a black hole you would almost certainly be torn apart by the strong gravity. But it is *just* possible that you might be able to travel through the black hole to another time or even another universe!

LIFE IN THE UNIVERSE

If there is life elsewhere in the universe, it could look like almost anything. Think of the differences between a jellyfish and an eagle—yet these creatures both live on Earth. If creatures from the same planet can be so different, we can only imagine how weird a creature from an alien world might be.

Life can survive for long periods in space. Germs on a camera lens sent to the moon in 1967 were revived when they were returned to Earth two years later. But has life evolved on other planets? In 1996, there was a sensation when a piece of rock from Mars was found to contain what seemed to be the fossils of bacteria. Most scientists now doubt that these were actually ever living things. But future missions to Mars will concentrate on the search for the remains of life that may once have existed there.

▲ A greatly magnified image of part of a rock from Mars. Color has been added to show what some scientists think might be a fossilized Martian life-form.

The astronauts who went to the moon were put into quarantine when they came back, in case they had picked up any alien germs on their trip.

Aliens on Earth?

The distances between stars are so enormous that travel between them must be something that only the most advanced civilizations—if any—can manage. Although many claim to have seen them, there is no real evidence that aliens have visited the Earth, or that they exist at all.

▼ An idea of what intelligent aliens might look like

Some scientists think that there might be thousands of intelligent civilizations in our galaxy.

LISTENING FOR ALIENS

Since 1960 there have been several projects searching for radio signals from creatures from other worlds. In 1967, astronomers in England thought they had been contacted by aliens. They were receiving regular beeping radio signals from far out in space. These mysterious beeps were called "LGM" (Little Green Men) signals—but it was found that they were produced naturally by a pulsar. These strange spinning objects send beams of radio waves sweeping through space.

In the 1990s, a project called Phoenix was started—to listen for signals from a thousand stars. There are billions of stars in our galaxy, many with planets going around them, so there may be life out there. But only advanced civilizations would have the technology to transmit signals we could detect on Earth.

◄ Despite reports of UFOs, there is no real evidence that alien spacecraft have ever visited Earth.

▲ The Arecibo radio telescope that has been used to send messages into space in the hope that aliens will answer

When we send radio or TV signals, they travel out into space. They have reached thousands of stars already—so aliens could be watching our TV programs even now!

So far, no alien messages have been received by these projects—except perhaps for one mysterious signal picked up in 1977, called the "wow" signal (because a scientist wrote "wow" on the printout when he saw it). It was a sudden burst of radio waves lasting for over a minute that no one has been able to explain.

A powerful radio signal was sent from a radio telescope at Arecibo, Puerto Rico, in 1974. This digital signal was directed at a cluster of stars known as M13, with the aim of delivering a message about who we are and where we live. The message will take 25,000 years to reach its destination, even though it is traveling at the speed of light.

COSMIC QUESTIONS

Galaxies

We don't know quite why stars are grouped into galaxies. Galaxies have a range of forms, from delicate spirals to shapeless clumps. Our solar system is part of a spiral galaxy called the Milky Way. In a galaxy like ours, there are always some stars forming while others are fading away or blowing up. But some galaxies are full of stars that, for some reason, are all being born at once. These are called starburst galaxies.

It is thought that billions of years ago, most of the galaxies in the universe were blue—full of newly formed blue stars that have now faded away.

◀ A spiral galaxy 36 million light-years away. Our own Milky Way galaxy must look similar to this.

◄ This X-ray glow reveals the presence of a gas cloud. It is thought that "dark matter" keeps the cloud from breaking up.

Dark Matter

One of the biggest mysteries about the universe is that there doesn't seem to be enough of it! Scientists know roughly how much material there is in our part of the universe, because the gravitational pull of the material affects the way galaxies move. But they can find only about a tenth of this amount. The remaining nine-tenths is known as "dark matter," but the nature of this dark matter is a mystery. Some people think that part of the dark matter might be tiny dark stars, called "brown dwarfs," that are too dim for us to detect.

One theory is that dark matter is made of tiny particles called WIMPs! (which stands for Weakly Interacting Massive Particles).

An Expanding Universe

Since its birth, between 12 and 15 billion years ago, the universe has been expanding. We know this because, wherever we look, groups of galaxies are moving away from each other. Until recently, most scientists thought that the expansion of the universe would eventually stop and then everything would start to collapse into a "Big Crunch." But recent measurements of distant galaxies have shown that they are not slowing down as expected. It may be that some strange force is pushing them apart. But, whatever the reason, it seems that the universe will probably go on expanding forever.

The universe is millions of times older than the oldest human being.

◄ Each of these spheres represents the whole universe at a different stage of its development, with groups of galaxies getting farther apart.

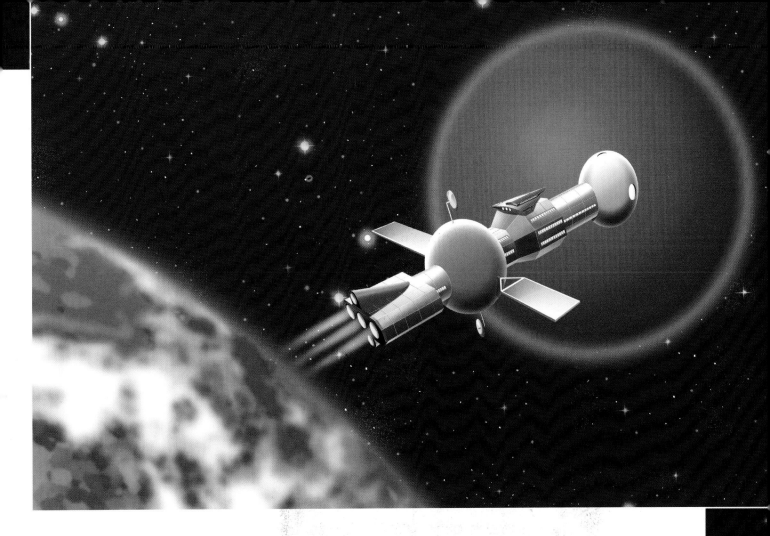

▲ Eventually the sun will swell up and destroy all life on Earth. But by then we may have spaceships that can travel to other stars and find new places to live.

The Earth is about 4.6 billion years old.

The End of the Universe

Eventually all the stars will run out of fuel and cease to shine. The universe will get darker and colder, until there is no light and almost no heat left. Long before this time, all life on Earth will have ended. The sun will swell up into a "red giant" and either swallow the Earth or burn away its surface. After this, what is left of the sun will gradually fade into darkness.

Whether or not the human race will be able to survive somewhere else in the universe is another mystery . . .

GLOSSARY

Asteroids Rocky objects like small planets, mostly found between Mars and Jupiter.

Atmosphere The layer of gases surrounding a planet.

Black hole A region in which gravity is so strong that not even light can escape from it.

Canyon A valley formed when a river wears away the ground.

Comet A lump of rock and ice whose orbit sometimes brings it close to the sun.

Galaxy A group of between a million and a trillion stars.

Hemisphere Half of a sphere, such as the northern or southern part of the Earth.

Hubble A space telescope, launched in 1990.

Light-year The distance a ray of light travels in a year: more than 6 trillion miles (9 trillion km).

Meteorites Fragments of rock that fall on the Earth from space.

Moon An object that orbits a planet.

Orbit The path of one object around another in space.

Polar ice cap Icy region found in the coldest parts of Earth and Mars.

Pulsar A spinning object—the remains of a star—that sends out beams of radio waves.

Radiation A form of energy that travels through space, such as light or X rays.

Red giant A swollen star, near the end of its life.

Supernova A massive exploding star.

Universe Everything that exists.

Variable star A pair of stars that seem to change in brightness as they change positions.

White dwarf A tiny, dead star that gives off a dim light.

X rays A type of high-energy radiation capable of traveling through most materials.

FURTHER INFORMATION

Web pages:

http://ispec.scibernet.com/station/
asteroid.html
Asteroids and Meteoroids

http://www.jpl.nasa.gov/solarsystem/
The Solar System

http://comets.amsmeteors.org
Comets and Meteor Showers

Books to read:

Angliss, Sarah. *Cosmic Journeys: A Beginner's Guide to Space and Time Travel*. Copper Beech Books, 1998.

Becklake, Sue. *All About Space*. Scholastic, 1999.

Couper, Heather and Nigel Henbest. *Blackholes*. Dorling Kindersley, 1996.

Maran, Stephen and Jacqueline Mitton. *Gems of Hubble*. Cambridge University Press, 1996.

Pepper, Dennis. *The Young Oxford Book of Aliens*. Oxford University Press, 1998.

Simon, Seymour. *Destination: Jupiter*. William Morrow, 1998.

Places to visit:

National Air and Space Museum
7th and Independence Ave., S.W.
Washington, D.C. 20560
(202) 357-2700
www.nasm.edu

NASA/Kennedy Space Center
Kennedy Space Center, FL 32899
(407) 452-2121
www.ksc.nasa.gov

INDEX

All numbers in **bold** refer to pictures as well as text.

Picture acknowledgments:

The publishers would like to thank the following for allowing their pictures to be reproduced in this book: Bruce Coleman/Astrofoto 6, 13, 17, 24, 28; Popperfoto 10, 11; Science Photo Library *cover*, 9/Julian Baum 15/Lynette Cook 21/NASA 8, 9, 22, 27/David Parker 25/Space Telescope Science Institute/NASA 5, 7, 19, 20/Victor Habbick Visions 23/Mount Stromlo and Siding Spring Observatories 26; artwork by Peter Bull Art Studio 2, 4, 16, 18, 29; all other artwork from HWPL.